LADY GAGA

From Shy Kid to Superstar-
Biography For Kids

Donovan Watkins

TABLE OF CONTENTS

INTRODUCTION: WHO IS LADY GAGA

Lady Gaga is one of the most famous singers and performers in the world. She is known for her amazing voice, her bold outfits, and her big heart. But before she became a superstar, she was just a little girl with big dreams. Her real name is Stefani Joanne Angelina Germanotta. She was born on March 28, 1986, in New York City, which is a big city in the United States.

When she was very young, Lady Gaga loved music. She started playing the piano when she was only four years old. She also enjoyed singing and dancing around the house. Her parents saw how much she loved music, so they gave her lessons and let her perform in school plays. Gaga worked hard in school and practiced her music every day.

But growing up was not always easy for her. Some kids made fun of her because she was different. She liked to dress in her own style, and she didn't always follow what everyone else was doing. Sometimes people laughed at her or told her she wouldn't succeed. But Gaga didn't let their words stop her. She stayed true to herself and kept working hard. She believed that one day, people would listen to her music and understand who she really was.

She played music in small clubs and shared her voice with anyone who would listen. It wasn't easy at first. Many people said no to her. But she kept trying. Then, one day, everything changed. She released her first big song called Just Dance, and it became a hit all over the world. People loved her music, her energy, and her style.

After that, more hit songs followed, like Poker Face, Bad Romance, and Born This Way. These songs made her even more popular. She sang about being yourself and not being afraid of what others think. She told people it's okay to be different. Her fans, who are called Little Monsters, love her because she helps them feel brave and strong.

Lady Gaga also became an actress. She was in a movie called A Star Is Born, and she sang a beautiful song called Shallow. She won many awards for her singing and acting, including Grammys and even an Oscar. But even with all her fame, she never forgot where she came from or the people who helped her.

She also started something very special called the Born This Way Foundation. This foundation helps kids and teens feel safe, loved, and proud of who they are. Gaga talks about being kind to others and being kind to yourself. She shares stories about times when she felt sad or scared, and how she got through them. She wants everyone to know that they are not alone.

Lady Gaga is not just a performer. She is a helper, a fighter, and a friend to many people around the world. She teaches us to love ourselves and to never be afraid of being different. Her story shows that you can follow your dreams, no matter how big they are. All it takes is hard work, courage, and believing in yourself.

Lady Gaga is a star, but she shines even brighter because of the love she gives to others.

Lady Gaga's journey teaches us something very important. Even when people say you can't do something, you can prove them wrong by believing in yourself. It's okay to be different. It's okay to dream big. Don't be afraid to be yourself. You are amazing just the way you are. Keep going, keep dreaming, and remember that you can do anything if you never give up.

CHAPTER 1: A SHY GIRL NAMED STEFANI

Before the world knew her as Lady Gaga, she was a little girl named Stefani. She was born in a big, busy place called New York City. Her full name was Stefani Joanne Angelina Germanotta. That's a very long name, isn't it? She lived with her mom, dad, and little sister in a small apartment filled with love, music, and laughter.

Stefani was quiet. She didn't talk a lot in school, and sometimes she felt nervous around other kids. She was shy, but not because she didn't care. In fact, she cared a lot. She was kind, polite, and always helped others. But deep inside, Stefani felt like she didn't always fit in.

She was different. While other kids liked playing tag or video games, Stefani liked playing the piano, writing songs, and dressing up in fun clothes. She didn't wear the same things as the other girls. Sometimes she wore shiny boots, big sunglasses, or hats that made people turn their heads. Some kids thought she was strange. They didn't understand her, and that made her feel alone.

But Stefani had something very special: her love for music. When she was just four years old, she sat down at the piano and started to play. It was like the piano spoke a secret language that only she could understand. She didn't just play notes—she played feelings. Happy ones, sad ones, even silly ones. She loved music so much that she would practice every single day.

Her mom and dad saw how talented she was. They gave her piano lessons and signed her up for music classes. Stefani also loved to sing. She would sing in the kitchen, in the shower, and even when she walked down the street. Her voice was soft at first, but it got stronger the more she used it.

At school, things weren't always easy. Some classmates teased her because she looked or acted differently. They didn't know how much their words hurt her. Sometimes Stefani cried when she got home. But even on the hardest days, she sat down at her piano and let her music help her feel better. Music was her safe place. It was where she felt strong, brave, and free.

She also started writing her own songs. She would sit with a notebook and write down her thoughts, her dreams, and even her worries. She turned them into lyrics—words that would one day become beautiful songs.

As Stefani got older, her love for performing grew. Even though she was shy, she joined school plays and talent shows. Every time she stepped on stage, something magical happened. It was like she became a new person. She was still Stefani, but she was braver, louder, and more confident. The stage felt like home.

She dreamed of becoming a star—not because she wanted to be rich or famous, but because she wanted to make people feel something with her music. She wanted kids like her to know they weren't alone. She wanted to help people smile, cry, dance, and believe in themselves.

At home, her parents cheered her on. They told her she could do anything if she worked hard and stayed true to who she was. They reminded her that being different was not something to hide—it was something to celebrate.

So Stefani kept going. She kept practicing the piano. She kept singing. She kept dreaming. She didn't let the mean words stop her. She didn't let fear win. She was still a shy girl, but she had something even stronger than fear: a heart full of music and a dream that never stopped growing.

Sometimes, the quietest people have the loudest dreams. It's okay to be shy. It's okay to be different. Just like Stefani, you can find something you love and let it help you shine. Whether it's music, drawing, sports, reading, or building things—your passion can be your superpower. Always believe in yourself, even when others don't. Keep going, keep growing, and never stop being you.

CHAPTER 2: MUSIC ALL AROUND HER

Stefani's home was full of music. It was in the air, in the walls, and in her heart. Her parents loved music, too. They played old songs on the radio, sang along in the kitchen, and danced around the living room just for fun. Her dad especially loved classic rock, and her mom enjoyed soft, beautiful songs. Stefani listened closely to every sound, every beat, every word.

She began to fall in love with all kinds of music. She liked pop songs that made her want to dance. She liked sad songs that made her feel deep emotions. She even liked opera, which is a type of music where people sing with very strong voices. No matter what the style was, music made her feel alive.

At home, Stefani spent hours at the piano. She didn't just play songs she learned from teachers—she also made up her own music. She pressed the keys softly when she felt calm, and loudly when she felt strong. She used music to tell stories without even speaking. Her fingers danced across the piano like they had a mind of their own.

When she wasn't at the piano, she was writing lyrics in her notebooks. Her notebooks were full of ideas, feelings, and dreams. Some songs were happy, some were sad, and some were full of wild imagination. She even wrote songs about monsters and outer space! Her mind was always creating something new.

Stefani also started singing more. She sang in the shower, in her room, and even while doing her homework. Sometimes she would pretend she was in a big concert, with thousands of fans cheering for her. She would twirl, jump, and strike poses like a true star. Even though no one was watching, she gave it her all.

At school, she joined the choir and acted in plays. One day, she even got a big part in a school musical. When she sang on stage, her voice filled the room. Everyone clapped and cheered. For the first time, many of her classmates saw how talented she was. Some of the kids who used to tease her were now impressed.

Music gave Stefani something very special—confidence. It made her feel strong, even when she was nervous. It helped her speak up, even when she was shy. When she made music, she felt like her true self.

She also liked helping other kids with music. If someone in the choir was nervous, she would smile and encourage them. If someone made a mistake, she would say, "It's okay. Let's try again." She wasn't just a good musician—she was a good friend, too.

One day, Stefani told her parents, "I want to do this forever. I want to make music for the rest of my life." Her parents smiled. They already knew. They believed in her, and they promised to support her every step of the way.

So, Stefani kept going. She took more music classes. She performed in more shows. She kept writing songs, dreaming big, and sharing her gift with the world. Music wasn't just something she liked—it was a part of who she was.

When you find something you love, like music, art, dancing, reading, or sports, hold on to it. Let it make you smile. Let it help you grow. Just like Stefani, you can use your passion to build confidence, feel happy, and help others. You don't have to be perfect. You just have to keep trying, keep learning, and keep doing what you love. Your special gift is meant to shine—so let it shine bright.

CHAPTER 3: BIG DREAMS, BIG STEPS

Stefani had a dream. It was not a small dream. It was big—very big. She wanted to become a music star. She wanted to sing her own songs on big stages. She wanted people all over the world to hear her voice and feel something special. Most of all, she wanted to be herself and help others feel strong by being themselves too.

But dreams don't come true overnight. They take time, practice, and hard work. Stefani knew that. So, she kept working. She kept learning. She told herself, "If I want my dream to grow, I have to take big steps."

One of the first big steps she took was going to a special high school for the arts. It was a school where students studied music, dance, and acting. Everyone there loved performing, just like she did. For the first time, Stefani felt like she truly belonged. She made friends who also had big dreams. They cheered each other on, practiced together, and helped one another get better.

At this school, Stefani studied very hard. She practiced piano every day, worked on her voice, and even learned about music history. She stayed after school to write songs and help with performances. While other kids might have gone to the mall or watched TV, Stefani stayed focused on her dream. She didn't mind. Music made her happy.

Even when she was tired or felt unsure, she kept going. Sometimes she didn't feel good enough. Sometimes she got nervous before a show. But she never let fear stop her. She remembered how music made her brave when she was younger, and now it helped her again.

Stefani also began performing in small places outside of school. She sang in coffee shops, tiny theaters, and school events. There weren't big crowds, but every performance mattered. She gave her best each time. Some people clapped. Some people didn't understand her style. But she didn't give up. She knew that every step she took was bringing her closer to her dream.

As she grew older, Stefani began thinking about her future. She wanted to go to college, but not just any college. She wanted to go to a music school that would help her become a true artist. She worked hard and got accepted into a top music program in New York City. She was excited—but also scared. It was another big step.

At college, things were harder. She met many talented people, and sometimes she felt like she wasn't good enough. But instead of quitting, she worked even harder. She kept writing songs, performing, and learning. She never forgot why she started—because music was her passion, and she had a dream to share it with the world.

But one day, Stefani made a bold decision. She wanted to follow her dream even more fully. So, she left college early to start her music career. It was a risky move. Some people didn't understand. But Stefani trusted her heart. She believed in herself. She was ready to take her next big step.

There would be challenges. There would be failures. But she was not afraid. She was ready to work, grow, and keep moving toward her dream—one brave step at a time.

Dreams can be big, and that's okay. You don't have to do everything at once. Just take one step at a time. Work hard. Be brave. Keep learning. Even if others don't believe in your dream—believe in yourself. Just like Stefani, you can turn your passion into something powerful. Don't be afraid to try, to grow, and to shine. Every big dream starts with one small step.

CHAPTER 4: SINGING FROM THE HEART

Stefani was ready to follow her dream. She had left college because she believed in herself and wanted to become a real music artist. Now, it was time to make her dream come true. But it wasn't easy. In the beginning, no one gave her a big stage. No one handed her a record deal. She had to start from the bottom.

She performed in small clubs in New York City. Some of the places were tiny and not very fancy. Sometimes only a few people were there to watch. But that didn't stop her. Stefani sang with all her heart, just like she always had. She gave her best at every show, even if only five people were listening. She smiled, she danced, and she sang her songs with deep feeling.

She wrote her own songs, too. She didn't want to just sing what other people wrote. She wanted her songs to come from her own life, her own feelings, and her own thoughts. Her songs were about being different, about being strong, about love, and about not giving up. Some songs were fun and made people dance. Others were emotional and made people think. Every song came from a real place in her heart.

At the same time, Stefani started to create her own style. She didn't want to look or act like everyone else. She wore big bows, glittery jackets, shiny boots, and wild wigs. Sometimes she even made her clothes by hand. She had a big imagination and wanted to show the world her creative side. People started to notice her not just for her music but also for her unique fashion.

Some people didn't like it. They said she looked too strange or too different. But Stefani didn't listen. She said, "I was born this way." She believed that everyone should feel free to be themselves, no matter what others think. She wanted her fans to feel proud of who they are, just like she was proud of herself.

One day, a music producer saw her perform and believed in her talent. He worked with her on recording songs and helped her share them with more people. Soon, she started getting attention from music companies. She worked very hard to make her first album. It took time, patience, and many hours in the studio, but she never gave up.

When her first songs came out, people loved them. Her music was different, fun, and full of energy. One of her first big songs was called "Just Dance." It became very popular and played on radios everywhere. People loved her voice, her message, and her look. She had finally made it. She had become a real pop star.

From then on, Stefani started using the name Lady Gaga. It came from a song called "Radio Ga Ga" by the band Queen. She loved how the name sounded and how it felt. Lady Gaga was more than just a name. It was a part of her personality. It showed her boldness, her power, and her creative spirit.

Even as Lady Gaga became more famous, she never forgot where she came from. She still sang from the heart. She still wrote her own songs.

She still wanted to make people feel something special. She believed that music could help people feel strong, happy, and proud of who they are. Every time she stepped on stage, she gave her best.

Lady Gaga was not just a singer. She was a storyteller, a performer, and a light for people who felt different or left out. She showed the world that being yourself is not only okay—it's amazing. Her music helped people feel brave. It helped them feel seen. And it all started because she chose to sing from her heart.

Always be true to who you are. Whether you're singing, drawing, writing, or playing, do it with love and honesty. When you follow your heart, people will notice. Don't worry if others think you're different—that's what makes you special.

Just like Lady Gaga, you can make a difference by being yourself. Keep shining, keep dreaming, and never stop sharing your heart with the world.

CHAPTER 5: TRYING, FAILING, AND TRYING AGAIN

Before Lady Gaga became a superstar, her life was full of ups and downs. She had big dreams of becoming a famous singer, but it didn't happen right away. In fact, her journey was filled with many hard moments. There were times when people didn't believe in her. There were times when she didn't win. And there were times when she felt like she was all alone.

When she first started trying to make music her career, Lady Gaga worked very hard. She wrote songs late at night. She practiced singing every single day. She played her piano until her fingers were tired. She performed in small clubs where only a few people showed up. She wore creative outfits to stand out, hoping someone would notice her. She gave everything she had. But even with all that hard work, success didn't come quickly.

One day, she finally got a big break. A music company signed her and said they wanted to help her make music. Lady Gaga was so excited. She thought her dream was finally coming true. But then something surprising and sad happened. The music company changed its mind. They told her she wasn't right for them, and they dropped her from their team.

Lady Gaga felt heartbroken. She had worked so hard, and now it felt like all of that work didn't matter. She cried. She felt hurt. She wondered, "Am I good enough? Should I stop trying?"

But instead of quitting, Lady Gaga made a brave choice. She wiped her tears and said, "No. I won't stop. I believe in me." That's what made her special. Even when the world said no, she still said yes to herself. She got back up and tried again.

She went back to the small clubs and kept performing. She wrote more songs. She practiced even harder. She worked with new music producers and made new friends who believed in her. One of those producers was named RedOne. Together, they made music that sounded fresh and exciting. They believed they could make something great.

Even then, not everyone said yes. Some people still said no. Some people didn't understand her style or her music. But Lady Gaga didn't stop.

She kept going. She kept trying. And finally, one of her songs, "Just Dance," was picked up by a music company. This time, it was different.

"Just Dance" became a hit. People all over the world were dancing to her song. Suddenly, the girl who was once told she wasn't good enough was now being played on radios, shown on TV, and talked about by millions. She had done it. She had turned failure into success.

But Lady Gaga always remembers the times when things didn't go right. She says those moments made her stronger. They taught her to be patient, to work harder, and to keep believing. Every time she failed, she learned something new. And every time she got back up, she became stronger.

She wants her fans to know that it's okay to fail. Everyone fails sometimes. What matters most is that you don't give up. You try again. And again. And again. Because every time you try, you get a little better. And one day, just like Lady Gaga, you might reach your dream too.

It's okay to fall down. What matters is that you stand back up and keep going. Failing does not mean you are weak. It means you are learning, growing, and getting closer to your dream. Just like Lady Gaga, you can do great things if you don't give up. Believe in yourself, even when it's hard. You are stronger than you know, and your dreams are worth chasing—one step at a time.

CHAPTER 6: ACHIEVEMENTS

Lady Gaga's hard work and dreams finally paid off in a big way. She went from singing in small clubs to becoming one of the most famous singers in the world. But her success didn't happen overnight. It took a lot of effort, and she didn't give up—even when things were tough.

One of her first big achievements was her debut album, called The Fame. It was filled with songs that made people want to dance. Songs like "Just Dance" and "Poker Face" became huge hits. People all over the world started listening to her music. They loved how different her style was. She wasn't afraid to be herself, and that made her stand out. The album went on to sell millions of copies, and Lady Gaga became a global superstar.

Lady Gaga didn't just stop there. She kept pushing herself to do even more amazing things. She worked on her second album, The Fame Monster, which had even more hits. One of the biggest songs from that album was "Bad Romance," a song that became known everywhere. It was a song about love, but with a twist. It had a catchy beat and powerful lyrics that made it fun to sing and dance to. People couldn't stop listening to it.

As her fame grew, Lady Gaga began to collect awards. She won Grammys, which are some of the most important music awards in the world. She received awards for Best New Artist, Best Dance Recording, and Best Pop Vocal Album, just to name a few. Her fans were so proud of her. And Lady Gaga was proud of herself, too. She worked hard for these awards, and they showed that she was one of the best in the music world.

But Lady Gaga's achievements weren't just about music. She became a role model for people around the world. Her message was clear: be proud of who you are, no matter what others say. She wanted everyone to know that it's okay to be different. In fact, being different is what makes you special. People admired her courage to speak up about things that matter. She stood up for equality, kindness, and the right to be yourself.

One of Lady Gaga's greatest achievements was starting the Born This Way Foundation, which helps young people be confident and stand up for what they believe in. The foundation supports mental health, kindness, and acceptance. It encourages everyone to be proud of who they are, no matter where they come from or what they look like. Lady Gaga wanted to make the world a better place for all kids, just like her.

Lady Gaga didn't just achieve success in the music world. She became a person who changed the world with her kindness, her messages, and her example. Her fans looked up to her not just for her music, but for the way she made them feel. She showed them that they were not alone. She made them feel strong, proud, and ready to take on anything.

Your achievements are not just about what you win or how many awards you get. They're about how hard you work and how you stay true to yourself. Lady Gaga achieved so much because she never gave up, and she always believed in her dreams. You can do the same! Keep working, keep believing, and remember, your achievements are waiting for you, too. Be proud of who you are and keep moving toward your dreams. Anything is possible if you never stop trying.

CHAPTER 7: HELPING OTHERS ALONG THE WAY

As Lady Gaga's fame grew, she never forgot the importance of helping others. She realized that with her success, she had the power to make a difference in the world. She didn't just want to be known for her music; she wanted to use her voice to help people who were struggling or who didn't feel accepted.

One of the biggest ways Lady Gaga helped others was through her Born This Way Foundation. This special foundation is all about helping kids and young people feel proud of who they are. It helps them build confidence, share their feelings, and learn how to take care of their mental health. Lady Gaga knew that many kids didn't feel like they fit in, and she wanted to change that. She wanted to remind everyone that it's okay to be different and that we should all accept each other.

The Born This Way Foundation works on many different projects. It talks about how important it is to be kind to one another, to help those who are feeling sad or lonely, and to make sure everyone feels loved. Lady Gaga has always said that kindness is one of the most important things we can give to others. She's used her fame to bring attention to causes that make the world a better place, like ending bullying and making sure everyone has the right to feel safe.

Lady Gaga also helps by speaking out about mental health. Mental health is about how we feel inside. Sometimes, people feel sad, worried, or scared, and that's okay. But it's important to talk about these feelings and ask for help when you need it. Lady Gaga has shared her own struggles with mental health to show people that they're not alone. She wants everyone to know that it's okay to ask for help, and it's okay to take care of your mind just like you take care of your body.

Another way Lady Gaga helps is by being a friend to her fans. She calls them her "Little Monsters." She talks to them online, shares messages of hope, and even invites them to her concerts. She makes sure they know that no matter what happens in their lives, they have a friend in her. Lady Gaga believes that everyone deserves to feel loved and accepted, and she makes sure to remind her fans of this every day.

Even though she is a famous singer, Lady Gaga never forgets where she came from. She uses her success to make life better for others. She gives money to charity, helps raise awareness for important causes, and encourages everyone to treat others with respect and kindness.

Lady Gaga's work reminds us all that no matter how big or small we are, we can always make a difference. She shows that when we help others, we create a world where kindness and love are shared by everyone. She teaches that helping others is one of the best ways to live a happy and meaningful life.

You don't have to be famous or rich to help others. Just like Lady Gaga, you can make a big difference by being kind and supportive. Every time you smile at someone, share a kind word, or stand up for someone who needs help, you're making the world a better place. So, keep being kind, and always help others along the way.

CHAPTER 8: COSTUMES, COLORS, AND CREATIVITY

Lady Gaga is known for more than just her incredible music. She's also famous for her bold and creative style. When you think of Lady Gaga, you might imagine her wearing something wild or colorful. That's because she has always loved expressing herself through fashion. Her costumes, makeup, and hairstyles are a big part of who she is as an artist.

From the very beginning of her career, Lady Gaga knew she wanted to stand out. She didn't want to wear the same clothes as everyone else. She wanted to be unique, and she wanted her clothes to tell a story. Every outfit she wore was like a piece of art. She wore everything from giant dresses made of bubbles to shiny, futuristic costumes. Sometimes, she wore outfits that were so strange that people couldn't believe their eyes! But that was the point. She wanted people to be surprised and to think differently about what fashion could be. Lady Gaga's outfits have always been about more than just looking good; they are a way for her to make a statement and share her ideas with the world.

One of Lady Gaga's most famous costumes is the "meat dress." She wore it to an awards show, and it got people talking. The dress was made of real meat! People were amazed, shocked, and even confused, but Lady Gaga didn't care. She didn't dress to please others; she dressed to express herself and her ideas. To her, the meat dress was a statement about how women are sometimes treated like objects instead of being seen for their talents. It made people stop and think about the world in a different way. Even though some people didn't understand it, the meat dress became an unforgettable moment in Lady Gaga's career, and it showed her fans that it's okay to be bold and to challenge what is considered "normal."

Another way Lady Gaga shows her creativity is through her makeup and hair. She has worn every hair color you can imagine—pink, blue, blonde, and even green. Her makeup is often bold and dramatic. She's not afraid to wear bright red lipstick or paint her face in wild colors. Her look changes all the time, and that's because she likes to have fun with it. For Lady Gaga, makeup is just another way to express her personality and creativity. It's like putting on a costume every day, depending on how she feels. Sometimes, she wears her hair in big, wild styles, and other times, she goes for a sleek, modern look. She changes her style based on the message she wants to send or how she wants to feel that day.

Lady Gaga's creativity isn't just about her clothes and makeup. She also loves to tell stories with her music videos. Each music video is like a mini movie, with exciting costumes, dramatic scenes, and unexpected surprises. She uses these videos to show her fans how she's feeling or to send a message to the world. For example, in the video for "Bad Romance," Lady Gaga wears beautiful but strange costumes, and the video is full of powerful imagery. The setting is dark and mysterious, and the video tells a story about love, struggle, and the desire for something more. It's clear that Lady Gaga loves to create and make art that is full of meaning. Each music video is a chance for her to show her creativity in a new way, and she uses it to share her ideas with her fans.

Even when Lady Gaga is not in front of the camera or on stage, her creativity is still alive. She often collaborates with other artists and designers to create new and exciting things. She works with fashion designers to come up with clothes that no one has ever seen before, and she works with makeup artists to create unique looks that match her vision. She loves to be involved in every part of the process because she knows that creativity is about teamwork and sharing ideas. It's not just about what one person can do on their own—it's about working with others and learning from each other to make something amazing.

But Lady Gaga's creativity isn't just about the way she looks or the art she creates. It's about the way she lives her life. She is always thinking outside the box, and she encourages her fans to do the same. She wants everyone to know that it's okay to be different. In fact, being different is what makes you special. Lady Gaga teaches her fans that the most important thing is to be yourself, no matter what anyone else says. When you're true to yourself, you can create the most beautiful and unique things in the world.

Lady Gaga's creativity has inspired millions of people around the world. Her fans look up to her because she's not afraid to be bold, to experiment, and to push the limits of what people expect. She teaches us that creativity is about finding your own voice and sharing it with the world. And if you're brave enough to be yourself, you'll find that the world will listen and be amazed by what you can do.

Just like Lady Gaga, you can be creative and express yourself in your own special way. Don't be afraid to try new things, wear what makes you feel happy, and show the world who you really are. Remember, being creative isn't about following the rules—it's about being true to yourself and having fun with your ideas. Your imagination is your superpower, so let it shine! You can be as bold and creative as you want to be, and the world will be excited to see what you create.

CHAPTER 9: FANS AROUND THE WORLD

Lady Gaga isn't just famous in one country—she has fans all over the world! People from every corner of the globe love her music, her style, and the messages she shares. She's a superstar who has brought together millions of people, no matter where they come from or what language they speak. Her fans, called "Little Monsters," feel like they are part of something special because Lady Gaga always makes them feel important.

Lady Gaga's fans are from every age, race, and background. Whether they're young or old, everyone can find something in Lady Gaga's music that speaks to them. Her songs talk about love, strength, and the power of being yourself. That's why so many people feel connected to her music. It's not just about the beats and melodies—it's about the way her songs make people feel. They remind her fans that they are not alone and that they should always be proud of who they are.

One of the best things about Lady Gaga's fans is how supportive they are of each other. The "Little Monsters" are like one big family. They help each other through tough times and celebrate each other's successes. When a fan is having a hard day, they can turn to the Little Monsters community for encouragement. Lady Gaga has made it clear that she wants her fans to support one another, to be kind, and to lift each other up. Her message is simple: "We are all in this together."

Lady Gaga is also very active in connecting with her fans. She doesn't just perform on stage and then disappear—she wants to stay close to her fans. She talks to them online, shares messages of love and hope, and even invites them to her concerts. At her shows, she makes sure to talk directly to the crowd, reminding them how much they mean to her. Whether she's performing in New York City, London, or Tokyo, Lady Gaga always makes sure that her fans feel like they're part of the show. She tells them that they are the reason she keeps going, and that without them, she wouldn't be where she is today.

When Lady Gaga performs, she doesn't just sing and dance. She creates an experience for her fans. Her concerts are full of exciting lights, costumes, and performances that take her fans on a journey. She wants her shows to be a place where everyone can be themselves and have fun. It's a space where no one has to feel judged, and everyone can enjoy the music together. That's why so many people look forward to seeing her perform—they know it will be a magical experience they won't forget.

Even though Lady Gaga is one of the most famous people in the world, she never forgets about her fans. She regularly sends them messages of love, reminding them to stay strong and true to themselves. She's also worked with her fans on projects like the "Born This Way Foundation," where they come together to spread kindness and fight bullying. Through this foundation, Lady Gaga helps her fans feel supported and encouraged to be the best versions of themselves.

Lady Gaga's fans are always there for her, just like she is there for them. She says that her fans are her greatest strength, and that their love and support help her through tough times. They are the reason she keeps creating and sharing her music with the world. Lady Gaga's fans show us that when we come together and support one another, we can do amazing things.

You don't need to be a celebrity to have a great group of friends who support you. Just like Lady Gaga's fans, you can find people who lift you up and remind you how special you are. Remember, you are never alone. If you believe in yourself and treat others with kindness, you will always find people who will support you. You can

create your own "fan club" by being a good
friend and always spreading love and positivity
wherever you go.

CHAPTER 10: FUN FACTS ABOUT LADY GAGA

Lady Gaga is not only famous for her incredible voice and style, but there are many interesting things about her that make her even more amazing! You might already know a few things about her, but here are some fun and exciting facts that will help you understand her better. These facts show how creative, talented, and inspiring she is. Let's take a look at some of the things that make Lady Gaga so special!

1. Her Real Name Isn't Lady Gaga
You might think Lady Gaga is her real name, but it's actually a nickname she chose for herself. Her real name is Stefani Joanne Angelina

Germanotta! It might be surprising, but Lady Gaga thought that the name "Lady Gaga" sounded fun and exciting, and she decided it would be perfect for her pop star identity. She got the name from the song "Radio Ga Ga" by the band Queen. Now, the name Lady Gaga is so famous that most people don't even know her real name!

2. She Can Play the Piano

Lady Gaga's talent isn't just about singing. She is also a talented musician who can play the piano! She started playing the piano when she was only four years old, which is amazing! She can play many different types of music, including classical, jazz, and pop. Her love for the piano helped her write many of her hit songs. In fact, if you listen carefully to many of her songs, you'll hear the beautiful sound of her piano. She also uses the piano to express her feelings and connect with her fans.

3. She Loves to Write Songs

Lady Gaga is not just a singer; she's also an incredible songwriter. She writes most of her own music, and she loves doing it! She draws inspiration from her life, her emotions, and the world around her. Some of her songs are about love and happiness, while others talk about struggles and challenges. Through her songs, Lady Gaga connects with her fans in a deep way. She helps people feel understood and not alone, and that's one of the reasons her music is so powerful.

4. She Was on TV Before Becoming Famous

Before Lady Gaga became a huge star, she made a few appearances on television. When she was

19 years old, she had a small role on the popular TV show The Sopranos, which was about a mob family. Even though she wasn't famous yet, Lady Gaga always knew she wanted to be a star. She worked hard to get noticed and performed at small clubs and shows to build her career. She didn't give up on her dreams, and it eventually led her to becoming the superstar she is today!

5. She Loves Fashion

Lady Gaga is known for her bold, unique fashion sense. She loves wearing fun, unusual outfits that make her stand out. Whether she's wearing a huge dress made of bubbles or a sleek, futuristic outfit, Lady Gaga's style always catches people's attention. But did you know that she also designs some of her own costumes? She's worked with top fashion designers around the world, but she always makes sure that her outfits match her personality. She likes to have fun with fashion and isn't afraid to wear something completely different from what everyone else is wearing. For Lady Gaga, fashion is another way to express herself and show off her creativity.

6. She Loves Animals

Lady Gaga has a big heart, and that includes loving animals! She has a pet French Bulldog named Asia, and she loves sharing pictures of her with her fans. Lady Gaga is an animal lover and often talks about the importance of treating animals with kindness and respect. She also uses her fame to raise awareness for animal rights and the well-being of animals around the world. Her love for animals shows that she cares about more than just her career; she wants to make the world a better place for everyone, including animals.

7. She Has Won Many Awards

Lady Gaga is one of the most awarded artists of all time! She has won many Grammy Awards, American Music Awards, and even an Academy Award (Oscar)! She's worked incredibly hard to achieve her dreams, and her hard work has paid off. Winning these awards is a huge honor and shows that people recognize her talent and dedication to her music. But Lady Gaga doesn't take the credit for her success alone. She always thanks her fans for supporting her and helping her reach the top. She knows that she wouldn't be where she is today without the love and encouragement from her fans around the world.

8. She Was in a Movie

Did you know Lady Gaga isn't just a singer? She's also a talented actress! Lady Gaga starred in the movie A Star Is Born alongside Bradley Cooper. In the movie, she played a singer named

Ally, and her performance was so amazing that she won several awards. People were amazed by how well she acted, and it showed that Lady Gaga isn't afraid to try new things and challenge herself. She proved that she is not just a pop star—she is also an actress with a lot of talent.

9. She Loves to Help Others

One of the most inspiring things about Lady Gaga is how much she cares about helping others. She started the Born This Way Foundation to help young people who are struggling with mental health issues. The foundation encourages kindness, self-love, and acceptance. Lady Gaga wants everyone to know that it's okay to be different and that we should always treat others with kindness. She believes that by helping each other, we can all make the world a better place.

10. She Has an Amazing Voice

Lady Gaga is known for having one of the most powerful and beautiful voices in the world. She can sing in many different styles, from pop and jazz to opera. Her voice is so strong and unique that it's one of the things that make her stand out as an artist. She works hard to take care of her voice so that she can keep singing and performing for her fans. Whether she's performing on stage or recording a new song, Lady Gaga's voice always shines through, and that's part of what makes her music so special.

Lady Gaga's journey shows us that it's important to follow our dreams, work hard, and stay true to who we are. She's not afraid to try new things, make mistakes, and keep going. Just like Lady Gaga, you can achieve great things by being yourself, trying your best, and never giving up on your dreams. Remember, you have the power to be creative, kind, and unique—just like Lady Gaga. Keep being awesome, and don't be afraid to shine.

CONCLUSION: YOU CAN SHINE TOO

Lady Gaga's story is not just a tale of fame and fortune. It's a story about a young girl with big dreams, determination, and a passion for being herself. From her early days in New York City, where she worked hard to become the artist she is today, to the moment she took the world by storm with her incredible voice, unique style, and big heart, Lady Gaga shows us all that dreams are possible if we don't give up.

But what makes Lady Gaga truly special isn't just her music or her fame—it's the way she faced challenges and turned them into opportunities. She wasn't always the big star she is now. She faced rejection, criticism, and moments of doubt. There were times when it seemed like her dreams might not come true. But Lady Gaga didn't let those tough times stop her. Instead, she used them to fuel her passion and keep going. Every time she faced a setback, she learned from it, grew stronger, and moved forward with even more determination.

Through her journey, Lady Gaga has shown us that it's okay to be different. In fact, being different is something to celebrate! She didn't try to be like everyone else; instead, she embraced her unique qualities and used them to build her career and her identity. Her outfits, her music, her personality—they all come from a place of confidence and creativity. Lady Gaga has taught us that we don't have to follow the crowd or fit into a box. We can be ourselves, and that's enough.

One of the most important things we can learn from Lady Gaga is the power of kindness and helping others. She has used her fame and platform to raise awareness about important issues, like mental health, equality, and kindness. Her Born This Way Foundation encourages people to love themselves and embrace their uniqueness. She wants everyone, especially young people, to know that they are worthy and capable of achieving their dreams, just like she did. Lady Gaga's story teaches us that when we lift others up and help them along the way, we can all shine brighter together.

But you don't need to be a famous singer to make a difference or to be someone special. Just like Lady Gaga, you have your own unique talents, abilities, and gifts that make you amazing. You don't have to be perfect, and you don't have to have it all figured out. What matters is that you try your best, stay true to yourself, and keep moving forward. Everyone's path is different, and you may face challenges along the way—but those challenges don't define you. It's how you respond to them that makes you stronger and more resilient.

Just think about it—Lady Gaga was once a little girl with big dreams, just like you. She didn't know exactly how everything would turn out, but she took it one step at a time, believing in herself and working hard every day. She faced struggles, she had doubts, but she kept going. And look at her now! She's not just a pop star; she's a role model, an advocate for kindness, and an inspiration to millions.

So, what can you learn from her story? That you can shine too. Your dreams matter, and with hard work, dedication, and a belief in yourself, you can make them come true. Whether you want to be a singer, an artist, a scientist, a teacher, or anything else, the key is to keep trying, never give up, and stay true to who you are. Everyone has the potential to be great in their own way. You have the power to make a difference, to help others, and to create something amazing.

Remember, Lady Gaga didn't get to where she is by following the easy path. She made mistakes, she failed sometimes, but each time she got back up and tried again. That's what makes her story so inspiring: it's not just about success, it's about never giving up, no matter how tough things get. She proves that no dream is too big and no obstacle is too great if you believe in yourself and keep pushing forward.

Just like Lady Gaga, you can achieve amazing things. You have your own light, your own unique spark that the world needs. It doesn't matter where you come from or how old you are. If you keep going after your dreams, no matter how big or small, you will find your way to success.

So, the next time you face a challenge, remember Lady Gaga. Remember how she kept going, how she believed in herself, and how she always stayed true to who she is. You can do the same. You can shine just like she did, and your light will shine even brighter if you keep being yourself, following your heart, and never giving up on your dreams.

You've got this. You can do anything you set your mind to. Just remember to stay true to yourself, help others along the way, and keep shining. The world is waiting to see you succeed, and you have everything it takes to make your dreams come true, just like Lady Gaga did.

QUIZ TIME: HOW MUCH DO YOU KNOW LADY GAGA

Now that you've read all about Lady Gaga's journey and achievements, it's time to see how much you've learned! Test your knowledge with these fun questions:

1. What is Lady Gaga's real name?
   - a) Stefani Joanne Germanotta
   - b) Stephanie Smith
   - c) Gaga Johnson
   - d) Joanne Lady

2. At what age did Lady Gaga start playing the piano?
   - a) 2 years old

- b) 4 years old
- c) 10 years old
- d) 12 years old

3. What famous song did Lady Gaga get her name from?
   - a) "Bohemian Rhapsody"
   - b) "Bad Romance"
   - c) "Radio Ga Ga"
   - d) "Poker Face"

4. Which movie did Lady Gaga star in with Bradley Cooper?
   - a) A Star Is Born
   - b) The Hangover
   - c) The Hunger Games
   - d) Titanic

5. What is the name of Lady Gaga's foundation that helps promote kindness and mental health?

- a) The Born This Way Foundation
- b) The Lady Gaga Foundation
- c) The Fame Foundation
- d) The Kindness Foundation

6. What animal does Lady Gaga have as a pet?

- a) A dog named Asia
- b) A cat named Luna
- c) A bird named Charlie
- d) A rabbit named Fluffy

7. Lady Gaga is known for wearing creative and unique outfits. Which of the following is a famous Lady Gaga costume?

- a) A meat dress
- b) A flower crown
- c) A superhero costume

- d) A pirate outfit

8. What song made Lady Gaga a superstar and became an international hit?
    - a) "Just Dance"
    - b) "Million Reasons"
    - c) "Poker Face"
    - d) "Shallow"

9. What type of music does Lady Gaga often mix into her songs?
    - a) Jazz and opera
    - b) Country and rap
    - c) Rock and pop
    - d) Hip hop and reggae

10. What is Lady Gaga's message to her fans through her music and actions?
    - a) Be like everyone else

- b) Be kind to others and embrace your uniqueness
    - c) Always follow the rules
    - d) Only care about winning awards

Bonus Question:

11. Where is Lady Gaga originally from?
    - a) Los Angeles, California
    - b) New York City, New York
    - c) Miami, Florida
    - d) Chicago, Illinois

ANSWERS

1. a) Stefani Joanne Germanotta

2. b) 4 years old

3. c) "Radio Ga Ga"

4. a) A Star Is Born

5. a) The Born This Way Foundation

6. a) A dog named Asia

7. a) A meat dress

8. a) "Just Dance"

9. a) Jazz and opera

10. b) Be kind to others and embrace your uniqueness

11. b) New York City, New York

How did you do? Whether you got every answer right or just learned a few fun facts, remember that just like Lady Gaga, you can shine by being yourself and always reaching for your dreams.